MY LIFE TURNING POINT

आशुतोष अग्रवाल

THIS STORY DEDICATE TO MY LIFE

Contents

Preface

This idiosyncratic and episodic collection of stories reflects a life filled with love and adventure, both cerebral and physical. I have been extraordinarily blessed to have loved two exquisite women and, amazingly, to have been loved by them. At the same time I tried not to miss any opportunity for challenge and for adventure. If I have a regret, it is that in the pell-mell rush to achieve and experience, I sometimes did not wait to adequately consider what was really important, namely my relationships with those close to me. Herein I have tried to acknowledge those mistakes.

I have always believed that exploration is a way of life and whether in science or in the outdoors one mode of exploration enriches the other. In the words of some anonymous poet:

> ``I have travelled through great beauty
> To some measure of understanding
> You cannot ask for more than that."

History also tells us that peace does not come easily. That it takes vigilant international cooperation. In this regard I made it my policy to place all that I learnt on the internet to be freely available to all who wish to use that knowledge. This policy was founded on two coupled beliefs. First that the most effective way to roll back the limits of knowledge is to share it as widely and freely as possible. And second that through the process of sharing knowledge we achieve a mutual respect and cooperation that is to the benefit of all mankind. For this reason we must do all we can to resist all attempts to place censorship on that marvellous new means of communication and education that we call the Internet.

Acknowledgements

"Thanks to everyone on the Scribe team who helped me so much. Special thanks to Ellie, the ever-patient Publishing Manager, my amazing Scribe, the greatest cover designer I could ever imagine.The world is a better place thanks to people who want to develop and lead others. What makes it even better are people who share the gift of their time to mentor future leaders. Thank you to everyone who strives to grow and help others grow.

I want to thank EVERYONE who ever said anything positive to me or taught me something. I heard it all, and it meant something.All the dudes I ever slept with, I appreciate the experiences, but I ain't naming none of you.I want to thank God most of all, because without God I wouldn't be able to do any of this.

I SPECIALY THANK YOU TO MY SISTER WRITER MAHIMA BANSAL FOR MAKING MY BOOK COVER .

ONE SPECAL THANK YOU TO AMAR BHAI OUR 3AM CLUB OWNER FOR MAKING MY STORY TITLE ."

Prologue

ONE
MY LIFE INFORMATION

I was born in a small family, don't think it's a small family, but I live alone with my parents in a city called Gwalior and they named me ashutosh(kannu), why? Being with him is because of Mahadev. My parents must have had high hopes from me that I will study well, but what do they know, if I am born on a Sunday, then I am considered to be a jerk, but it is not like that, I am good at my studies and in sports as well.

TWO
MY LIFE

My life is going very well, we used to play a lot in childhood, watch TV, eat food and sleep, this is the routine of the day and most of all,I can make one friend her name raja udheniya bhut we dont know in fucture we make bestfriend and we live longer yarri in fucture & our both parents also be good friends.

At this time my father also used to tell everything to my best friend and he would have saved me from my mother. then i always told my father that when i'm become big person i will help poor people for making non-profit private hospital for free checkup ots my dream and they always this dreams come true when you working hard and studing hard bhut that time I'm not recognise that sentence.

THREE

MY SCHOOL LIFE IN SHORT

when i was living my own house i will join my uncle school name ramshree india international school(RIIS) bhut i failed to join that school bhut school principle are very good they say i will gift you can join bhut want to study one class back and if you are study well and get first division so i will promoted you to direct to 4th class next and i will achive that achivement after that class and i will more happy.

FOUR

MY LOVE LIFE IN SCHOOL & COACHING

IN SCHOOL I GOT MY FIRST CRUSH IN CLASS 2TH I KNOW U COULD DONT BELEIVEIT BHUT I TELL HER NAME MEGHA SHARMA, BHUT I WANT TO SAY U SOMETHING A BANIYA BOY WILL ALWAYS LOVE WITH OTHRER CAST GIRL BEACUSE THEY SCARED THAT IF WE MAKE GF AND THIS GIRL MEET IN FAMILY RELATION SO OUR PARENTS GIVE 90DEGRE IN HOUSE HAHAH....

SORRY FOR DISCONTINU THE STORY SO I'M COMING ON THIS POINT THAT WHEN I WILL GET MY CRUSH I WILL ALWAYS SEE MY CRUSH IN WHOLE TIME AND I ALSO FEEL THAT SHE ALSO LIKE ME BECAUSE WHEN I HAVE FIGHT WITH SOME GUY THEY WILL SAVE ME AND THEY TAKE REVENGE FOR MY FIGHT AND THEN I WILL HAPPY ALWAYS BHUT AFTER SOME TIME HER FATHER TRANSFER IN ANOTHER COUNTRY AND I LOST MY FIRST CRUSH THAT TIME .

WHEN I PROMOTED NEXT CLASS I LOST OUR MEMORY AND GOT STUDY HARD AND EVERYTHING GOES WELL BHIUT WHEN I REACH CLASS 6 TH I GOT MY SCEOND CRUSH & YOU NOT KNOW I WILL BECOME VERY HAPPY FOR JUST BECAUSE MY CRUSH LIVING IN NEAR MY HOUSE AND HER MOM WERE MY CLASS TEACHER HIHIHI.....,

BHUT I DONT KNOW THAT THIS CRUSH ALSO NOT MY REAL LOVE, BHUT I DONT KNOW THAT MY ALL EFORTS FOR SERCHING REAL LOVE ARE WORTHLESS AND I WILL LEAVE THIS BEACUSE I SONT FINE REAL OVE IN THIS GIRL. And i went further in my LIFE .

BHUT I GOT ONE MORE TWIST IN MY COACHING I GOT ONE MORE CRUSH BHUT IS BAAR BANIYA HAI AND After a long time, the ghost became a friend after having an idea, AND AFTER SOME DAYS SHE GETS MY HELP BECAUSE SOME PEOPLE ARE TROUBLING HER AND HE SAY PLZZ LEAVE ME AT MY HOUSE AND I GOT ERY HAPPY FOR THINK HER BHUT ITS ALSO NOT IN MY KISMAT.

SPECIAL PART OF THIS STORY

HOW A BOY CHANGED HIS LIFE FOR SOME SPECIAL GIRL ,BHUT WHEN THWY LEFT WHAT WILL HAPPEN IN NEXT PAGE.

FIVE

PART 1 TWIST PART OF THE STORY

IN THIS PART YOU GET SOME MASS MASALA

SO LETS START ITS'S ABOUT THAT TIME WHEN I WAS IN

CLASS 11TH AND I GOT MY FIRST REAL LOVE IN LIFE WITH SPEACLE GIRL NAME NIHARIKA FROM AGRA BHUT STUDY WITH ME IN MY SCHOOL (RIIS GWALIOR), AND FIRST TIME GO SHAMMED TO TELL HER DIRCT THAT I LIKE U AND I DONT HAVE ANY IDEA THINK TO HOW TO MAKE HER MY LOVE AND SUDDELY I GOT IDEA FIRST MAKE HER SMALL BRO. MY BEST BEST JUNIOR FREND AND I STRUGLE 2 YEARS AFTER MY 12 EXAM I FIND HER IN MY TOWN BHUT I DIDN'T RECOGNISE HER,

AND FINALY I ASK HER BROTHER WHATS NIHARIKA SOCIAL ID AND THEY GAVE ME HER ID AND I SEND REQ. I GENRALLY WAIT TO ACCEPT BHUT ITS BEEN LONG TIME AFTER 2 MONTHS LATER SHE ACCEPT MY ID AND START TALKING EACH OTHER IN DAY AND NIGHT BHUT THEY DONT KNOW I LIKE HIM SUDDENLY.

I START THAT TOPIC AFTER 3 MONTHS AND BEING I'M IN TRAIN I PROPOSE HER AND SHE WILL CONFUSED WHAT TO DO AND I GAVE HER 2 DAYS TIME AND SHE WILL CALL ME NORMALY IN 22'NOV19 WE TALK NORMALY AND I CHANE HER NIKE NAME BECAUSE HER NIKE NAME MATCH WITH MY SIS. AND AFTER THAT AFTER SOME DAYS.

I SUFFER SOME POOR DAYS BEACUSE MY FATHER HEALTH CONDITION VERY POOR AND ADMITIED IN HOSPITAL IN FARIDABAAD AND THAT TIME MY HOLE FAMILY LIVE IN MY BUA'S HOUSE AND MY BROTER NAME KAPIL BHAIYA WILL HELP ME EVERY WERE IN EVERY CONDITION

,SO MY RELATION WERE GOING TO BE VERY HARD CONDITION WE TALK EACHER LIKE WE WAKE UP GOT VEDIO CALL EACH OHTER AND NIGHT TIME 2AM TO MORNING 5AM , BHUT WHEN I WAS MEET WITH HER I GOT MY LOCKDOWN IN HERE AND MY WISH WILL STAY ENDED,BHUT IN LOCKDOWN I GOT MY FIRST BRKUP WITH HER AND I GET FEEL BAD BHUT SHE MAKES NEW BF AFTER FEW DAYS AND AFTER SOME DAYS MY FRIEND NAME VIKRANT WILL HELP ME TO PACHTUP WITH MY LOVE BHUT YOU WILL NEVER KNOW IN THIS RELATIONSHIP.

I GETS 8 BRKUPS WITH HER ,LETS COME ON POINT AFTER 2020 LOCKDOWN WILL END IN THE MONTH OF DEC. AND I GOT PALNED THAT I WANT TO MEET HER IN ROORKEE(NEAR HARIDWAR 500KM FAR AWAY) AND I WILL GOING THIS PALCE IN 18 ' MARCH 2021 TO GIVE HIM SUPRICE AND I GAVE HIME CHOCOLATE WHEN WE MEET EACH OTHER WE SPENT 1-2 HRS,

IN THERE AND THEY WERE GAVE EXCUSE THAT HE GETS CALL FROM COLLEGE TO MEET TO TAKE ADMIT CARD AND THEN TEY GO HOUSE AND GET SLEEP AND I HAVE TRAIN MORING BHUT I NOT TO WAKE EARLY AND I MISSED MY TRAIN AND I TELL HER THAT I MISSED MY TRAIN SHE COULD NOT BELEIVE ME WHEN GET VEDIO CALL THAT CAN THEM BELIVE AND CAME FOR ME AND TAKE TO THE BESTI NAME NIDHI SHARMA BOYFRIENDS HOUSE TO REST HERE AND HER BF NAME RAJAT SAINI AND THEY BRING ME LUNCH IN HOTEL AND THEN .

I WILL RESERVATION MY NEXT BUS TO BACK MY HOME TOWN AT 5PM,AND THEN THEY CALL ME I WILL MAKE YOU DINNER FOR U FOR TRAVEL AND I SAY NO BHUT SHE SAY I MAKE MY OWN HAND AND THEN I COUDNOT REFUSED AND SHE WIL GIVE WATER BOTTLE AND DINNER IIN BUS STAND AND FINALY LEAVE THERE TOWN .

AFTER SOME WEEK WE GOT SERIOUS MATTER THAT I SAYS HER THAT PLZZ TELL MY SELF TO YOUR PARENTS BECAUSE I TELL MY PARENTS FOR OUR REALATIONSHIP AND THEY WERE SAY YES BHUT SHE WERE SCRAED TO TELL TELL HER PARENTS AND THAT TIME SHE DECIEDED TO GIVE ME EXCUSED FOR BRKUP WITH ME (I GOT MARRIED WITHIN 2MONTHS & WE FINALLY OVER BETWEEN US) AND THEN .

I GOT MENTAL DEPRESS BEACUSE I GAVE MY TIME 2.5 YERAS TO THIS GIRL . I WILL REFUSED ALL STUDY FOR THIS GIRL AND THEN THEY SYAS THAT I GOT MENTALY, AND THEN I DECIDED TO SEND HER GIFT I ORDER A GIFT FOR HER LIKE HAPPY MARRIED LIFE MY LOVE (SONG MERE YAAR KI SHADDI HAI).

THEN I GOT BIG MISTAKE FOR ER AND MY ALSO THAT WE DESTORY OUR RELATIONSHIP SUCH I GOT MENTAL LOVE HER BHUT I DIDN'N GET CONTROL ON MY MIND AND THEN I TALK TO HER FATHER THAT WE BOTH ARE IN REALATIONSHIP SINCE 2.5 YEARS HE SAY YOU ARE LIE I TELL HER I SEND YOU SOME PICS OF MY RELA.

AND THEN THEY GIVE ME TREATS ON CALL AND I DIDN'T GET THAT NIHARIKA ALSO GET SOME FATHER NE THAPAD MARE HAI BHUT.

AND AFTER SOME TIME I REALSIED I GOT A BIG MISTAKE AND IN THE MORING HER MOTHER AND FATHER CALL ME AND SAY HOW WOULD YOU LIKE THIS AND I SAY WHAT DIDN'T MEAN YOU THEN THEY SAYS YOU BOTH ARE DOING SEXCUALY ACTIVITES AND WE BOTH SAY NO ITS WRONG DECISION OF YOURS AND AFTER FEW TIME THEN THEY RELISED ME AND NIHARIKA SAY RIGHT AND

WE BOTH ARE WRONGS.

AT THIS TIME WE BOTH ARE STAY ALONE AT THAT TIME I GO IN HAVY DEPRESSION AND HAVY STRESS AND AT THAT TIME MY LIFE GOES TRUNING POINT SAYS WHAT YOU CHOSE DEP. & LIFE FORWARDING AND I WILL CHOSE FORWARDING BHUT SAYS THAT REALY LOVE WILL NEVER FORGET THAT WILL HAPPEN WITH ME IN EVERY TIME

NEXT PART COMING SOON ....

She Came After Few Year In My Life As A Friend

bhut know she was very happy and i will always want to be happy

Shyari

1) BHO PYAR HI KYA JISME ASHIQ JUDA NA HUYE HO,

OR BHO IQSH HI KYA JISME DIL TOOTE HI NHI HO||

Thank You All For Reading My Book

HELPING HAND

1. MAHIMA BANSAL(SISTER) FOR MAKING DESIGN COVER PAGE

2. AMAR BHAI (FRIEND) FOR HELP TO MAKE STORY TITLE

3. NIHARIKA (EX LOVE,BUDDY) FOR EDIT COVER PAGE